RAINBOW WORLD

Poems from Many Cultures

Edited by Debjani Chatterjee
and Bashabi Fraser

Illustrated by Kelly Waldek

HODDER
Wayland

Copyright in this collection © Debjani Chatterjee and Bashabi Fraser 2003
Illustrations copyright © Kelly Waldek 2003
Book copyright © Hodder Wayland 2003

Published in Great Britain in 2003
by Hodder Wayland, an imprint of Hodder Children's Books
This paperback edition published in 2004

Project editor: Katie Orchard
Designer: Jane Hawkins

The right of Debjani Chatterjee and Bashabi Fraser to be identified as the editors
and Kelly Waldek as the illustrator of this work has been asserted by them in accor-
dance with the Copyright, Designs and Patents Act 1988.

British Library Cataloguing in Publication Data
Rainbow World: Poems from Many Cultures
Children's poetry
I. Chatterjee, Debjani II. Fraser, Bashabi
808.8'1

ISBN: 0 7502 4281 7

Printed and bound in Great Britain by Clays Limited, St Ives plc.

The paper and board used in this paperback by Hodder Children's Books are natural
recyclable products made from wood grown in sustainable forests. The manufacturing
processes conform to the environmental regulations of the country of origin.

Hodder Children's Books
A division of Hodder Headline Limited
338 Euston Road, London NW1 3BH

Introduction

Ours is a 'rainbow world', full of rich colour, amazing diversity
and natural beauty. As poets and editors, we wish to celebrate
our world through a variety of poems from many lands. This
multicultural anthology focuses on the voices of Asian and Black
poets from Britain, the Caribbean, Australia, New Zealand and
the continents of Asia and Africa. Under each poet's name we have
indicated the part of the world from which they come. In many
cases there is more than one geographic label as poets travel and
embrace more cultural identities.

Rainbow World is a collection of well over a hundred poems by
more than 80 poets, including such well known voices as those of
Nobel Laureates Rabindranath Tagore and Derek Walcott. We have
chosen themes to reflect experiences, loves and even dreams. The
themes range from 'Who's Who?' which expresses cultural and
racial identity to 'Who Sings for Fathers?' which focuses on the
intimacy of close relationships, and from 'Hip Hip Hurrah!' which
looks at celebrations, to 'Tree in the Heart', which explores the
mysterious world of myth and magic. To paraphrase the words of
Tagore, we want our book, 'to bring the distant near, in friendship,
and to make a brother or a sister of the stranger.'

Debjani Chatterjee   Bashabi Fraser

Contents

WHO'S WHO?

race, culture and identity

The Perfectly Baked Cakes

You're not black or white
you're YELLOW
'Perfectly baked'
from the middle of the oven
in the Chinese myth.
Well that certainly explains a lot.

Bekleen Leong
(South Africa and UK)

Airmail to a Dictionary

Black is the mellow night
Without the black there would be no white.

Black is the pupil of the eye
Putting colour in the sea's skin and earthen sky.

Black is the oil of the engine
On which this whole world is depending.

Black is light-years of space
Holding on its little finger this human race.

Black is the colour of ink
That makes the History books we print.

Black is the army. Wars in the night
Putting on the black to hide the white.

Black is the colour of coal
Giving work to the miners and warmth to the cold.

Black is the strip upon my cardcash
That lets me get money from the Halifax.

Black is the shade of the tree
Sharp in definition against inequality.

Black is the eclipse of the sun
Displaying its power to everyone.

Black is the ink from a history
That shall redefine the dictionary.

Black is a word that I love to see
Black is that, yeah, black is me.

Lemn Sissay
(Ethiopia and UK)

Who's Who

I used to think nurses
Were women,
I used to think police
Were men,
I used to think poets
Were boring,
Until I became one of them

Benjamin Zephaniah
(Jamaica and UK)

Their Plan

Who says
  I should wear a skirt

Who says
  The Earth is dirt

Who says
  I should look like you

Who says
  I should do as you do

Who says
  It's time to eat

Who says
  I should eat meat

Who says
  I should comb my hair

Who says
  The best is 'fair'

I am
  What I am
I'll do what
  I can
To destroy
  Their plan

Sista Roots
(Caribbean and UK)

11

a 'coloured' girl,
I sleep with rainbows

In the belly of the night, when people shed
their skins like snakes and become the cord
that fuses them to fluid dark, I will stand
in prisms of azure and vermilion.
I, a coloured girl with limbs alive with light,
will find gold in the cup of my hand
and in the arch of my foot the strength
to bear heaven.

   Nigger is a word of bullet consonants.
In my dreams the word will heal itself –
jagged black letters opening up like children's hands …

I am black. I am white.
I am the colour of the sun at noon.
I breathe with the sea.

For coloured girls who sleep with rainbows
there is light in the spittle of strangers.
My father, as black as brown can be;
my mother, as white as the half-moons in his nails.
I am their tangible kiss.

I will see my father
in the painting of my shadow on the earth,
my mother in the light which is the paintbrush.
I will dream again of brilliant distinctions
which span the sky with colour we reach
up and further up to see.

Lucinda Roy
(UK)

All in the Name
(an acrostic)

Debonaire,

Elegant,

Brilliant,

Jovial,

All describe me very well.

Not accurately, perhaps, but

In my dreams I am all these and more.

Debjani Chatterjee
(India and UK)

What Colour is a Kiss?

(a mulatto song)

Because we are not black,
because we are not black,
the black man questions what we say,
declares we held him back.

Because we are not white,
because we are not white,
the white man questions what we say,
declares we sapped his might.

Because we do not claim
home elsewhere in the world
we claim no foetal foreign fame
in ancient matrix curled.

Because we do not want
another land but this,
nor care about the tints of skin,
(what colour is a kiss?)

we put out searching hands
to reach, to touch another,
to hold the neighbour in our love,
to know and keep a brother.

A. L. Hendriks
(Jamaica)

Note: A mulatto is someone of mixed European and African parentage.

Truth

In every person
There lives a person of true identity
Untarnished by society.
It is the person you sleep with
When you sleep alone.
And when no one is talking to you
She talks endlessly, sensibly, truthfully.
Secret minutes mirror staring
Reflect the self that is hidden.
This is the person who helps you to dress up,
Fills you with confidence
To a ridiculous level,
Without which you would not survive.
So don't imitate –
Pretence is a game
That is only safe for two players.
You and the real you.

Su Andi
(UK)

Same But Different

My friend and I
travelled home together by night bus
My friend is white
As we parted at the station-stop
she said
that her fears
were of rapists and robbers
for me
that too
But as I walked the distance home
on pounding tiptoes
Each sudden shadow
was a threat of the National Front

Merle Collins
(Grenada and UK)

Africa

Africa my Africa
Africa of proud warriors in the ancestral savannahs
Africa of whom my grandmother sings
On the banks of the distant river
I have never known you
But your blood flows in my veins
Your beautiful black blood that irrigates the fields
The blood of your sweat
The sweat of your work
The work of your slavery
The slavery of your children
Africa tell me Africa
Is this you this back that is bent
This back that breaks under the weight of humiliation
This back trembling with red scars
And saying yes to the whip under the midday sun
But a grave voice answers me
Impetuous son that tree young and strong
That tree there
In splendid loneliness amidst white and faded flowers
That is Africa your Africa
That grows again patiently obstinately
And its fruit gradually acquires
The bitter taste of liberty

David Diop
(Senegal)

Tapestry

The long line of blood
and family ties
An African countenance here
A European countenance there
An Amerindian cast of cheek
An Asiatic turn of eye
And the tongue's salty accommodation
The tapestry is mine
All the bloodstained prints
The scatterlinks
The grafting strand of crinkled hair
The black persistent blooming.

Grace Nichols
(Guyana and UK)

WHO SINGS FOR FATHERS?

family and friends

A Card for Me Mom

It is Mother's Day tomorrow
and the shops are full of wonderful things –
candles, picture-frames, pot-pourri in glass dishes,
but I only have money for a card, and there are dozens –
cards with teddies and roses, cards with moms
in dresses, with gold and red hair and blue eyes.
None of them look like me Mom.
If there was just one card to show
Mom with her gold necklace, bangles and earrings,
reminding me of her soft jingle-jangle as she washes
the curry pots or mixes the dough for rotis and naans,
in her silk kameezes and chiffon chunnies – one mom
with long black hair and flashing dark eyes
who looks more like me Mom!

Bashabi Fraser
(India and UK)

Notes: A kameez is a long tunic dress worn by South Asian women
over a salwar (trousers).
Naan is baked bread from Pakistan and North India.
A chunni is a long scarf worn over a kameez.

Brendon Gallacher

For my brother Maxie

He was seven and I was six, my Brendon Gallacher.
He was Irish and I was Scottish, my Brendon Gallacher.
His father was in prison; he was a cat burglar.
My father was a communist party full-time worker.
He had six brothers and I had one,
   my Brendon Gallacher.

He would hold my hand and take me by the river
Where we'd talk all about his family being poor.
He'd get his mum out of Glasgow when he got older.
A wee holiday some place nice. Some place far.
I'd tell my mum about Brendon Gallacher.

How his mum drank and his daddy was a cat burglar.
And she'd say why not have him round to dinner.
No, no, I'd say, he's got big holes in his trousers.
I like to meet him by the burn in the open air.
Then one day after we'd been friends two years

One day when it was pouring and I was indoors,
My mum says to me: I was talking to Mrs Moir
who lives next door to your Brendon Gallacher.
Didn't you say his address was 24 Novar?
She says there are no Gallachers at 24 Novar.

There never have been any Gallachers next door.
And he died then, my Brendon Gallacher
Flat out on the bedroom floor, his spiky hair,
His impish grin, his funny flapping ear.
Oh, Brendon. Oh, my Brendon Gallacher.

Jackie Kay
(Nigeria and UK)

Isn't It ...

Isn't it true that mothers everywhere
Love to nag?
Don't do this, don't do that,
Scolding without stop.

Every morning when Mum goes to work
How happy my sister and I are!
Yet when she's late coming home from work
We rush to the kerb and wait and wait ...

Ke Yan
(China)

Water Everywhere

There's water on the ceiling,
And water on the wall,
There's water in the bedroom,
And water in the hall,
There's water on the landing,
And water on the stair,
Whenever Daddy takes a bath
There's water everywhere.

Valerie Bloom
(Jamaica and UK)

uncle boatman

my uncle
bes boatman in de world
hold oars like dey he arms

mammy say he don need oars
row good wid de hands

my uncle
make sail fill even if dere no wind
move boat through water
like big fish after guppies

mammy say he don need boat
he swim good as stingray

my uncle
catch crawfish wid old harpoon
bite head off electric eels
open beer bottles
wid de teeth

mammy
i say
how come he bite so well?

mammy finger her throat
say he ought be born barracuda
god make dreadful mistake

Caroline Carver
(Jamaica)

Once Upon a Time

Once upon a time, son,
they used to laugh with their hearts
and laugh with their eyes;
but now they only laugh with their teeth,
while their ice-block-cold eyes
search behind my shadow.

There was a time indeed
they used to shake hands with their hearts;
but that's gone, son,
Now they shake hands without hearts
while their left hands search
my empty pockets.

'Feel at home,' 'Come again,'
they say, and when I come
again and feel
at home, once, twice,
there will be no thrice –
for then I find doors shut on me.

So I have learnt many things, son.
I have learned to wear many faces
like dresses – homeface,
officeface, streetface, hostface, cocktailface,
with all their comforting smiles
like a fixed portrait smile.

And I have learnt too
to laugh with only my teeth
and shake hands without my heart.
I have also learned to say, 'Goodbye,'
When I mean 'Goodriddance';
to say, 'Glad to meet you';
without being glad; and to say, 'It's been
nice talking to you,' after being bored.

But believe me, son
I want to be what I used to be
when I was like you. I want
to unlearn all these muting things.
Most of all, I want to relearn
how to learn, for my laugh in the mirror
shows only my teeth like a snake's bare fangs!

So show me, son
how to laugh; show me how
I used to laugh and smile
once upon a time when I was like you.

Gabriel Okara
(Nigeria)

For the Mother

she

blazed

comet trails

from the oil

of her burning lamps

through the lonely vigil

of the night

dispelling

clouds of doom

she opened

trajectories

of sky

woven in her womb

she

rolled

away the stone

blocking an empty tomb

to prove

we are not here

we

are

risen

Jean 'Binta' Breeze
(Jamaica and UK)

Bulu's Freedom

She was a distant niece.
An only child of her parents.
Her father died when she was one
and her mother at three.
At four she was blinded
because there was no disinfectant
to wash down her eyes.
But she was a pretty, happy child
growing up with other children
in an extended family
in rural Bangladesh.

When she was about ten, I saw her
on one of my flying five-yearly visits
to the ancestral homestead.
She was talking with other children
glowing with excitement of kinship,
'He is my uncle ... from London ...
rich ... has a big car ...'
I moved out of earshot
in acute embarrassment.

She did not actually ask me for a thing!
Money, sweets, toys, a pretty frock ...
Nothing!

I only discussed these matters
perfunctorily,
with my cousin,
her legal guardian.

On my next visit
I heard she was dead.
Cholera got her.
She did not even have a grave.
Floods had washed down
the whole burial ground by the river
to the sea,
and to God.

Shafi Ahmed
(Bangladesh and UK)

Town and Village

Yes, people, I am home!
It is really myself,
Come and greet me.
Oh, grandmother, clap your hands for me,
Clatter your voice in greeting.
But, oh, I see you people.
I am glad; but sorrow too
For those I shall not see.

You see, people, these things I bring.
The shining bicycle for visiting my friends
Which the small boys will fall from
And learn to ride.
And see these blankets, dresses.
I am home with my presents
For all the people of this place
And none have been forgotten.

J.H. Chaplin
(Kenya)

Grandmother

You brought a heritage of songs and dreams, but they were
Left to decay within your open palms, as your children turned
Their faces from your dark gaze, and stopped their ears
   to your
Stories, longing only for their father's powerful pallor.

They let your name decay unused, smothered you
   with silence,
Ignored your presence and denied the very rumour of your
Life. So impoverished, I cannot search out your home, learn
Your stories nor hear your songs, or honour your faith.

Leaving me the only gifts of yours that denial could not
Quench. These rich tints of hair and skin that link me
Irrevocably to you. Mark me yours beyond dispute, Dark
Mother I walk in your skin. Your granddaughter at last.

Jeanne Ellin
(Anglo-Indian, UK)

Who Sings for Fathers?

they don't
suckle or nurture
cradle, cajole
sing nursery rhymes
tell stories
like Roald Dahl

they get bad press
as
thieves of childhood
violent
drunkards
who
attack their
own

a night down the pub
suits fathers

tell me your
father's story

how do you
remember his life?

can it be
neatly stated
in a sentence or two?

I never voiced my request
only gazed at
your father's
photograph
you kept on the wall
his smiling worn face
a
memory of my own
father's portrait
cigarette in hand
pencil-thin
moustache
hair groomed
charmingly suave

his life
before me

I wanted a song
for my father
would have brought
him flowers
and
sweet-smelling herbs
but I was always
afraid
they would wilt
in his presence
in the silence
he kept
as he sat
sipping on
unspent emotion.

Georgina Blake
(Caribbean and UK)

RAINBOW ALLIANCE

travel and landscape

Too Long I've Wandered ...

Too long I've wandered from place to place,
Seen mountains and seas at vast expense.
Why haven't I stepped two yards from my house,
Opened my eyes and gazed very close
At a drop of dew on a stalk of rice?

Rabindranath Tagore
(India)
Translated by William Radice

Postcard Poem: Solo

Mum, you needn't have worried one bit.
I travelled fine, fine, solo. Carried
in steelbird-belly of music shows.
I ate two passengers' pudding twice.
Nibbled nothings nutty and chocolatey.
Sipped cool Cokes. Had more nibbles.
All over mountain after mountain.
Over different oceans. Over
weird clouds, like snow hills
with trails of straggly shapes
drifting, searching. And strangers
talked – Germans going on big-fish hunt,
Italians to ride glass-bottomed boat,
a Dane to do snorkelling. Then, Mum,
I hopped from steelbird-belly, among
sun-roasted people of a palmtree place.
Welcome to Jamaica, voices called out.
Whole family hugged a sweating me
and took me off. Other exotics
got collected up in cars and coaches
to be naked on beaches, while
steelbird stood there shining-ready
for more come-and-go migrations.

James Berry
(Jamaica and UK)

Midsummer Tobago

Broad sun-stoned beaches.

White heat
A green river.

A bridge,
scorched yellow palms

from the Summer-sleeping house
drowsing through August.

Days I have held,
days I have lost,

days that outgrow, like daughters,
my harbouring arms.

Derek Walcott
(St Lucia)

Migrants

We migrated before we moved,
the gestures that we knew
were sown into new garments;
new words emerged
from our lips.
We learnt to drink
tea from cups
and water in glasses.
Knives and forks
replaced our fingers,
but the cuisine was stubborn
demanding its own etiquette.
Our shoes were laced,
neatly tied up
we were delivered
into the service of a new age
despairing of our inheritance.

We read comics, chewed gum
drank coke from bottles,
watched John Wayne shoot Indians
as we clapped.
Then Marilyn Monroe smiled.
Aftershave arrived
Hollywood style.
The radio blasted us with rock and roll
and we learned to dance
for a dollar or a dime
and signed our future on dotted lines.

We migrated before we moved;
the other place came to us.

Mahmood Jamal
(India, Pakistan and UK)

Adventurer

When I want adventure,
there is a place I go to.
I sit quietly, close my eyes
and I am away
among dragons, flying cats,
walking, talking fish
and an old woman in a funny hat
who grants my every wish.

John Lyons
(Trinidad and UK)

Arrival 1946

The boat docked at Liverpool.
From the train Tariq stared
at an unbroken line of washing
from the North West to Euston.

These are strange people, he thought –
an Empire, and all this washing,
the underwear, the Englishman's garden.
It was Monday, and very sharp.

Moniza Alvi
(Pakistan and UK)

Windrush Welcome

They brought a certain style
to the sceptred isle
from that other realm, the Caribbean.

One newspaper spoke of their dazzling ties
and said hope shone in their eyes.
But they came with no sword or musket.

I speak of those Windrush pilgrims, pioneers,
or simply call them followers of a dream
when dreams were coloured red, white and blue.

But like the all-embracing breeze
that shows no concern
for the origin of a flag
let the heart learn
to fly its banner
without regard to colour
as moon and dark unite
within a single sky.

On such a day
will black and white
raise a rum
to Windrush welcome
and a flag will open
out its fluttering arms
and this time round
the bard will say

This England, that was wont to conquer others
Hath made a glorious conquest of itself.

John Agard
(Guyana and UK)

Note: The SS *Empire Windrush* brought 492 West Indian emigrants
to Britain in 1948, the first major Caribbean migration to Britain
after the Second World War.

Between My Two Worlds

When I left London
I wrote of English summers
Of bluebells and blackbirds
And dreamt of the snow.

I came back to Scotland
And longed for the Monsoons,
The flocks flying homewards
In the deep sunset glow.

My mother's concern, my father's care,
My daughter's soft body that wasn't there;
So I switched my priorities and went back to stay
Carrying deep longings when I went away

To be enfolded in India
In its rich living spree,
Yet turning to Britain
In my memory;

Till the unexpected happened
And my worlds switched again
To experience long daylight
And pine for the rain

Of a country burning
With the sun and my pain
Of living between two worlds
That I cannot maintain.

While my mother falters
And my father grows old
I hold this, my country,
as my daughter holds.

Bashabi Fraser
(India and UK)

Note: Monsoon comes from the Arabic word *mausam*, which
means 'season', and is used in all Indian languages as such.
Monsoons refer to the seasonal rains that arrive in India in June
and retreat in October, travelling from south-east to north-west.

Traveller's Prayer

Is not de heavin' Lord
Is not de pushin' Lord
Is not de rockin' an' de
rollin' of de boat Lord

Is not de shiftin' Lord
Is not de tossin' Lord
Is not de jerkin' an' de
jumpin' of de boat Lord

Is not de liftin' Lord
Is not de fallin' Lord
Is not de driftin' an' de
skippin' of de boat Lord

Is not de grindin' Lord
Is not de choppin' Lord
Is not de tuggin' an' de
tossin' of de boat Lord

Is not de shovin' Lord
Is not de pushin' Lord
Is not de groanin' an' de
moanin' of de boat Lord

Is not de toin' Lord
Is not de froin' Lord
Is not de wonderin' if ah
goin' reach Port-of-Spain Lord

Is not movement ah waves Lord
Is de rhythm ah time Lord
Is de passin' an'
changin' ah de years Lord

Is de wonderin' Lord
Is de questonin' Lord
Ah leave it too long or thirty
years still not long enough Lord?

Amryl Johnson
(Trinidad and UK)

Tableau

My father is always standing on the deck
of the Bombay-England ship in '63,
looking back at his wife-to-be
since they were both 7,
arranged in a silk sari.

She waves farewell, then moves
to a thatched bungalow
amongst the palms of Juhu beach;
another life swinging on the verandah
seat with her books and
three children grow in the garden.

The ship docks in Tilbury.
Suitcases unpack days in college
and nights in Soho lodgings,
waking with the woman
at the Gateway to India.

Irfan Merchant
(India and UK)

World Geography and the Rainbow Alliance

Peking is in China
As Kingston is in Jamaica
As Delhi is in India
As nowhere, do we belong
You and I.

And should we ever run away
Where shall we run to?
And should we ever fight a war,
Who shall we fight for?
You and I.

At the end of the rainbow
Is a country of goodness
If we form an alliance,
Will we ever be free
To belong?

Or shall we always be carrying
Our ancestors' coffins in a bag?
Searching the globe
For a place to belong,
You and I.

Meiling Jin
(Guyana and UK)

HIP, HIP, HURRAH!

food, festivals and festivities

Bobolee

Good Friday,
like holy Granma Sundays.

Baptist shouters in long white cotton
walked like in funerals,
ringing bells,
singing hymns.
We waited for hen to cackle.
When we found her egg
we put the white in a drinking glass,
left it in Good Friday sun,
watched our future appear in pictures;

then the Judas rag doll,
as big as a man,
was dragged through the streets.

Every beating boy with a long stick,
'bolee, bolee, beat the bobolee,
bolee, bolee, beat the bobolee,'
beating towards the big fire waiting
for Judas in the stone quarry.

John Lyons
(Trinidad and UK)

Note: Bobolee is the name given in Trinidad to a Judas rag doll,
like a Guy Fawkes effigy, that is made at Easter and beaten by
children who shout: 'Bolee, bolee, beat the bobolee.'

Skanking Englishman
Between Trains

Met him at Birmingham Station
small yellow hair Englishman
hi-fi stereo swinging in one hand
walking in rhythm to reggae sound/Man

he was alive
he was full-o-jive
said he had a lovely
Jamaican wife
Said he couldn't remember
the taste of English food
I like mih drops
me Johnny cakes
me peas and rice
me soup/Man

he was alive
he was full-o-jive
said he had a lovely
Jamaican wife
Said, showing me her photo
whenever we have a little quarrel
you know/to sweeten her up
I surprise her with a nice mango/Man

he was alive
he was full-o-jive
said he had a lovely Jamaican wife

Grace Nichols
(Guyana and UK)

Curry Call

Curry red and curry hot
Curry in a steaming pot
Curry's aromatic smell
Curling down our cold stairwell
Making me sprint up the floors
And knock upon my neighbour's door!

Bashabi Fraser
(India and UK)

Hail Ramadan

Hail! Month of Ramadan.
Awakening to your call,
My heart blossoms;
A fountain of joy takes over my body,
I renounce my idleness
In awaiting your arrival.
I welcome you
With a thousand salaams.
With your holy touch
Wash away sins, guilt and sorrows.
Desiring to be rid
Of the regrets from a tainted past,
I embrace you.

Cast your forgiving glance
On the sins of this world.
I tell you that
Though one has everything,
Yet one feels a vacuum.

Kaiser Mustahab
(Bangladesh and UK)
Translated by the author and BWSG sisters

Notes: *Salaams* are salutations or greetings.
BWSG sisters are the Bengali Women's Support Group to which the
author and translators of this poem belong.

Mango

On Sunday afternoons in mango season,
Alleyne would fill his enamel basin
with golden-yellow fruit, wash them in clean water,
then sit out in the yard, under the grapefruit tree,
near the single rose bush, back to the crotons,
place the basin between his feet,
and slowly eat his mangoes, one by one, down to
    the clean white seed.
His felt-hat was always on his head. The yellow
    basin, chipped near the bottom,
with its thin green rim, the clear water, the golden fruit,
him eating slowly, carefully, picking the mango fibre
    from his teeth,
under those clear, quiet afternoons, I remember.
Me sitting in the doorway of my room, one foot on the
    steps that dropped
into the yard, reading him, over a book. That's how it was.

Robert Lee
(St Lucia)

Note: A croton is a type of Caribbean plant.

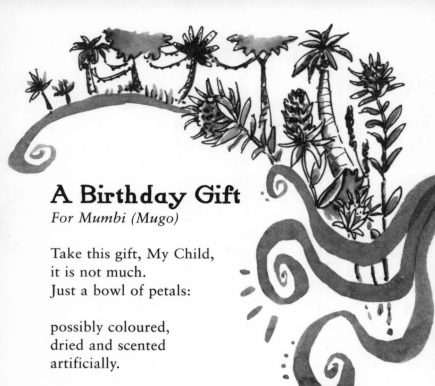

A Birthday Gift

For Mumbi (Mugo)

Take this gift, My Child,
it is not much.
Just a bowl of petals:

possibly coloured,
dried and scented
artificially.

It serves no purpose.

Except to bring
– when the breezes blow where they should,
which is rare these days –

a whiff of
old forest goodness and
modern garden freshness ... so called.

But enjoy it if you can.

In full knowledge that
it is just the kind of
not-so-useful gift

I would have loved
when I was then as
you are now.

Take this gift,
My Child,
it is for you.

Ama Ata Aidoo
(Ghana)

61

Airy Hall Iconography

The Tamarind hangs its head,
stings the eyes with its breath.

The Mango traps the sun by degrees,
transforms its rays into ambrosia.

The Coconut's perfect seal lets in rain,
bends with solid milk and honey.

The Guava is its own harvest,
each seed bound in fleshy juice.

The Guinep's translucence is all yours
if you skin its lips, chew its seed for the raw.

The Stinking-toe might be lopped off a stale foot,
on the tongue it does an about-turn: myrrh.

The Paw-paw runs a feather along your nose,
you want it to stop, you want more.

The Sour-sop's veneer is the wasp
treading air at the vaulted honeycomb.

The Sapodilla ducks you twice in frankincense,
you are fished out fighting to go down a third time.

Fred D'Aguiar
(Guyana and UK)

Notes: Airy Hall is a village in Guyana where Fred D'Aguiar
spent his childhood.
Iconography is the representation of a subject using symbols.
Tamarind, guinep, stinking-toe, paw-paw, sour-sop and sapodilla
are all fruit-bearing trees in the Caribbean.

The Savan Festival

Let us swing on the swing;
It's the Savan Festival in spring.
Mangoes are ripe, so eat
Them and the watermelons so sweet.
Mother's wheel is turning;
Pick up your cotton yarn for spinning.
The sandstorm is brewing.

Traditional Punjabi rhyme
(India)
Translated by Debjani Chatterjee

February

The month of February has twenty-eight days;
One day increases every fourth year.
That is true in all other countries or places
But, thanks to Ekushay, it's so different here:
February is the biggest month of our year.

Nirmalendu Goon
(Bangladesh)

Note: Ekushay February or 21 February is Bengali Language
Day and World Mother Language Day.

Corroboree

Hot day dies, cook time comes.
Now between the sunset and the sleeptime
Time of play about.
The hunters paint black bodies by firelight with
  Designs of meaning
To dance corroboree.
Now didgeridoo compels with haunting drone
Eager feet the stamp,
Click-sticks click in rhythm to swaying bodies
Dancing corroboree.
Eerie the scene in leaping firelight,
Eerie the sounds in that wild setting
As naked dancers weave stories of the tribe
Into corroboree.

Oodgeroo Noonuccal (Kath Walker)
(Australian Aborigine)

Note: A corroboree is a ceremonial gathering of aborigines.

Dance

Thud thud thud
  they bash their drums
Voices shriek out mumbled words
Faces as hard
  eyes as cold as a winter's night
Wooden bodies shift about like robots.

Don't you dance? they ask.

Of course we dance
We dance to the music
We dance to the rhythm
Music that touches the soul
Music that stirs the heart
Music that vibrates across the mountain tops.

Boom a boom a boompity boom
  the drums shout out
Ping zing ping a ling ting
  the steel pan and guitar echoes
Phew pheewp pheew pheewp the flute joins in.

A boom a boom a ping zing a ling pheewp
  a boompity boom,
They mingle
        they tingle
                they tangle,

Then the eyes laugh
  the face beams
The feet tap a rap a tap
  they tease the body
Together they dance and they dance,

Yes we do know how to dance
Do YOU?

Jean Buffong
(Grenada and UK)

Carnival Rhapsody

Beat dem drums
  Boys, beat dem drums,
   Fast and loud and sweet,
   Dey go ge we consolation,
   Dey go ease we sufferation,
   Down Frederick Street,
Down Frederick Street,

So beat dem drums
Boys, beat dem drums,
'Til Federation come
  Den we go jump in time
   To the Creole rhyme,
     Around de town.
        Around de town.

       And beat dem drums
       Boys, beat dem drums,
       'Til de Jour-Vert Monday comes
      When de Judge jump up,
    In de parson's frock,
      And de Doctor play de clown.

So beat dem drums
Boys, beat dem drums,
Look! Ah feel de rhythm in me spine,
Ah feel de rhythm,
In me chac-chac wine,
Shaking me far behind.

And beat dem drums
Boys, beat dem drums,
Ah feel de rhythm in me soul,
Ah feel de rhythm in me Creole blood,
E go stap wid me 'til ah ole.
E go stap wid me 'til ah ole.

Knolly La Fortune
(Trinidad and Tobago)

Mela Menagerie

It was summertime,
the animals were having a *mela*.
   The elephants cooked
curried pumpkin with *tikka masala*,
   sun-shy frogs and mice
sheltered under the hood of a cobra,
   bears and cockatoos
swapped couplets in a mini *mushaira*,
   horses and camels
pranced and danced a fantastic bhangra,
   tigers took pot-shot
at juicy papayas for one paisa,
   lions showed off paws
decorated with delicate henna,

donkeys for a laugh
crowned Mule their day-long Maharaja,
  pelicans swallowed
swords with mango chutney and *paratha*,
  Sinbad's ship sailed in
on waves of dolphin abracadabra,
  monkeys built bridges
recalling how they once helped Prince Rama,
  while Ali Baba
and forty rooks acted out life's drama.
  It was summertime,
the animals were having a *mela*.

Debjani Chatterjee
(India and UK)

Notes: In Urdu a *mela* is a festive fair in a marketplace; a
mushaira is a gathering of poets; a paisa is a coin used in India,
Bangladesh, Pakistan and Nepal; and *paratha* is a type of bread.

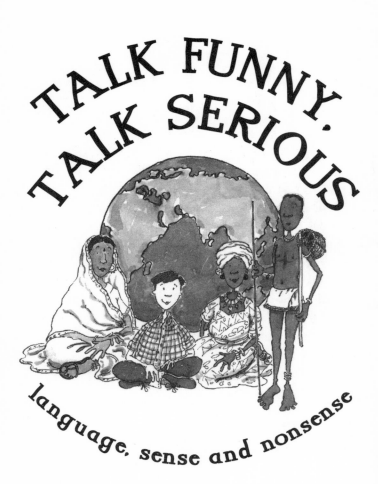

TALK FUNNY, TALK SERIOUS

language, sense and nonsense

Landing on the Moon

Gobble the news with seven grains
of alligator pepper, a pinch of salt,
white chalk, one sea-deep cry
for man's hike to Jehovah-hood, or,
must we not submerge in rituals
this explosive moment of animal triumph? –
Catch my hand, brother
we are annexing the kingdom of the gods.

Odia Ofeimun
(Africa)

Genius

I am a liric maniac
An urban Oral GENIUS
My style iz fast 'n' FURIOUS
Ma manna iz SPONTANEOUS
My lirix make yer laugh sometimes
As well as bein SERIOUS
I'll send yer round 'n' round the bend
I'll make yer act DELIRIOUS
Each word is hot, and can't be held
I suppose you'd say I'm DANGEROUS
I know I have a way with wurdz
The wurd I'd use iz NOTORIOUS
For those who want to challenge me
I find it quite RIDICULOUS
When critics try and put me down
Can't see them, they're ANONYMOUS
The only thing I have ter say
I see them all as ODIOUS
I luv my rithmz 'n' the beatz
Smell my wurdz, they're ODOROUS
I love my lirix to the max
Evry syllable 'n' sound iz MARVELLOUS
I execute my wurdz so well
I suppose you'd call it MURDEROUS
To work so hard on all these wurdz
Some say it is LABORIOUS
There's double meaning in my style
Four syllables ter you. AM ... BIG ... U ... OUS

I know I'm going on and on
But I certainly ain't MONOTONOUS
You have ter chill 'n' agree with me
The feeling is UNANIMOUS
Ter get inside yer head like this
I know that I am DEVIOUS
I do it in a sneaky way
I suppose I'd say MISCHIEVOUS
When pepul think about my rimez,
I know that they are CURIOUS
Don't understand the resun why
Becuz the cluez 'R' OBVIOUS
Okay you're right, my wurdz 'R' good
I suppose they are MIRACULOUS
Astounded by this type of rime
I know you 'R' OBLIVIOUS
There'z only one thing left ter say
I'm bad 'n' cool
'N' INFAMOUS

Martin Glynn
(Jamaica and UK)

Treat of a Sweet

Jelly A'Quiver shivered a shiver,
when sighting a sight of pure delight:
lolly pop slopping ice-cream topping.
It splashed it about, shouted a shout:
'A treat of a sweet for all to eat!'
With pineapple crushed, the cherries blushed,
orange segments smiled, peaches went wild,
macho pistachios grew moustachios,
walnuts and peanuts, but me no buts,
but melt with no trace, fruit and nutcase.

Debjani Chatterjee
(India and UK)

Sampan

Waves lap lap
Fish fins clap clap
Brown sails flap flap
Chop-sticks tap tap
Up and down the long green river
Ohe Ohe lanterns quiver
Willow branches brush the river
Ohe Ohe lanterns quiver
Waves lap lap
Fish fins clap clap
Brown sails flap flap
Chop-sticks tap tap

Tao Lang Pee
(China)

Note: *Ohe Ohe* means a swinging, swaying sound.

Body Talk

Dere's a Sonnet
Under me bonnet
Dere's an Epic
In me ear,
Dere's a Novel
In me navel
Dere's a classic
Here somewhere.
Dere's a Movie
In me left knee
A long story
In me right,
Dere's a shorty
Inbetweeny
It is tickly
In de night.
Dere's a picture
In me ticker
Unmixed riddims
In me heart,
In me texture
Dere's a comma
In me fat chin
Dere is Art.
Dere's an Opera
In me bladder
A Ballad's
In me wrist

Dere is laughter
In me shoulder
In me guzzard's
A nice twist.
In me dreadlocks
Dere is syntax
A dance kicks
In me bum
Thru me blood tacks
Dere run true facts
I got limericks
From me Mum,
Documentaries
In me entries
Plays on history
In me folk,
Dere's a Trilogy
When I tink of three
On me toey
Dere's a joke.

Benjamin Zephaniah
(Jamaica and UK)

Some of My Worst Wounds

Some of my worst wounds
have healed into poems.
A few well placed
stabs in the back
have released a singing
trapped between my shoulders.
A carrydown
has lent leverage
to the tongue's rise
and betrayals sent words
hurrying home
to toe the line again.

Lorna Goodison
(Jamaica and UK)

Mother Tongue

Yes,
I speak
Fluent
Urdu
But
In my dreams
I bawl,
Curse
And swear
In the
Queen's
English.

Hamid Shami
(Pakistan and UK)

My Loved One

Learn Maori my loved one,
it is the noble language of your ancestors
a great treasure from God.
Maintain it.
Lest it be lost my loved one.

Let the life stream of Waiwhetu cleanse you my son.
Let the house Te Aroha be the example of your pride
  my daughter.
Share it with all other kohanga
Maintain it lest it be lost my loved one.

Kuini Mohehau Reedy
(Maori, New Zealand)
Translated by the author

Notes: *Waiwhetu* is a place name: *wai* means 'water', and *whetu*
means 'stars'.
Te Aroha means 'the love'.
Kohanga means 'nest' and *reo* is the language nest where little children
are brought up speaking *te reo Maori* – the Maori language.

Phiniphin

The tide is in,
The tide is in,
The Phiniphin
Are out.
They love the sea,
The salty sea,
Of this there is
No doubt.

O watch them flip
And slip and slop
With clumsy hop
Right past
The sandy beach
Until they reach
The friendly shore
At last.

But when the tide,
The shifty tide
Stays right outside
The bar,
They can't go in
The Phiniphin;
The Phiniphin
Cannot go in:
They'd have to hop
Too far.

Frank Collymore
(Barbados)

83

The Joy of Fishes

Chuang Tzu and Hui Tzu
Were crossing Hao river
By the dam.

Chuang said:
'See how free
The fishes leap and dart:
That is their happiness.'

Hui replied:
'Since you are not a fish
How do you know
What makes fishes happy?'

Chuang said:
'Since you are not I
How can you possibly know
That I do not know
What makes fishes happy?'

Hui argued:
'If I, not being you,
Cannot know what you know
It follows that you
Not being a fish
Cannot know what they know.'

huang said:
Wait a minute!
et us get back
o the original question.
What you asked me was
"How do you know
What makes fishes happy?"
From the terms of your question
You evidently know I know
What makes fishes happy.

I know the joy of fishes
In the river
Through my own joy, as I go walking
Along the same river.'

Chuang Tzu
(China)
Translated by Thomas Merton

85

Hippo Writes a Love Poem to His Wife

Oh, my beautiful fat wife
Larger to me than life
Smile broader than the river Nile
My winsome waddlesome
You do me proud in the shallow of morning
You do me proud in the deep night
Oh, my bodysome mud-basking companion.

John Agard
(Guyana and UK)

ALL TOGETHER IN THE SUN

our animal world

There's This Goat

There's this goat –
Everyone says it's crazy
'Cause it eats
Whatever it can get
Clothes dried in the sun –
Maybe thinking it's a crispy pappadom,
The goat goes for it,
Chewing it with great delight,
Happily looking at everyone
With its shiny eyes,
Envelopes, postcards, the morning paper –
Stuffed inside its tummy
Make grumbling sounds;
Listening to the sounds with raised ears,
Counting them,
The goat walks around happily.

Begum Sufia Kamal
(Bangladesh)
Translated by Sajed Kamal

The Magnificent Bull

My bull is white like the silver fish in the river,
White like the simmering crane bird on the riverbank,
White like fresh milk!
His roar is like thunder to the Turkish cannon on the
  steep shore.
My bull is dark like the raincloud in the storm.
He is like summer and winter.
Half of him is dark like the stormcloud,
Half of him is light like sunshine.
His back shines like the morning star.
His brow is red like the back of the hornbill.
His forehead is like a flag, calling the people from
  a distance.
He resembles the rainbow.
I will water him at the river,
With my spear I shall drive my enemies.
Let them water their herds at the well;
The river belongs to me and my bull.
Drink, my bull, from the river; I am here
To guard you with my spear.

Traditional Dinka praise poem
(Sudan)
Translation

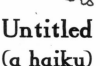

Untitled
(a haiku)

The falling flower
I saw drift back to the branch
Was a butterfly.

Moritake
(Japan)
Translation

All Day Long
(a tanka)

All day long having
buried himself
in the peonies,
the golden bee's
belly is swollen.

Okamoto Kanoko
(Japan)
Translated by
Kenneth Rexroth and Ikuko Atsumi

Notes: A *haiku* is a Japanese poem
of 3 lines.
A *tanka* is a Japanese poem of 5 lines.

Trapped in a Puddle

how long will you fight
little ant
before you are crushed?
surviving rocks and
oppressive jungle
you felt invincible
strode on the sands
of the great lake
mocking the hissing waves,
yet you cling to a stone
in its chuckling belly
while they reach caressingly
for your soul –
not even the printed page
floating so invitingly
can save you from wrath.

Amin Kassam
(Kenya and Uganda)

Mother Parrot's Advice to Her Children

Never get up till the sun gets up,
Or the mists will give you a cold,
And a parrot whose lungs have once been touched
Will never live to be old.

Never eat plums that are not quite ripe,
For perhaps they will give you a pain;
And never dispute what the hornbill says,
Or you'll never dispute again.

Never despise the power of speech;
Learn every word as it comes,
For this is the pride of the parrot race,
That it speaks in a thousand tongues.

Never stay up when the sun goes down,
But sleep in your own home bed,
And if you've been good, as a parrot should,
You will dream that your tail is red.

A. K. Nyabongo
(Ganda, Uganda)
Translation

Fly

ef a ketch im
a mash im
ef a ketch im
a mash im
ef a ketch im ...

Will you walk into my parlour
Said the spider to the fly
It's the prettiest snugliest parlour
That ever you did spy ...
And I
the fly
inspecting your web
this skein now then that
put my
microscopic eye
through its intricate weave
saw valleys of cloud
blue and serene
saw acres of grass
sheltered and green.
Ephemeral and light
I rested my life
and dazzled
I watched
You wove me inside
and dazzled
I slept
my chrysalis sleep .....

I woke up inside
no more dazzled and green.
Awake and alert
unfolding my wings
I stretched ... ...
But your skeins
not delicate now
resistant and strong
they wove me inside
I am trapped
I can't move
I can't butterfly
fly ... ...

And you
perched outside
your eyes large and clear
you see acres of green
you see valleys of cloud
you can move
you can fly ....
Now I look
through the web
I look into the void
I see numberless flies
training microscopic eyes
through intricate weave

94

ANANSI I cry
ANANSI – SI – SI I hear
the sky is too vast
how it scatters my cry
the sky is too clear
it hides my despair
they can't hear
they can't see
with their microscopic eye ....

ef a ketch im
a mash im
ef a ketch im
a mash im

A ketch im. im ... im

Velma Pollard
(Jamaica)

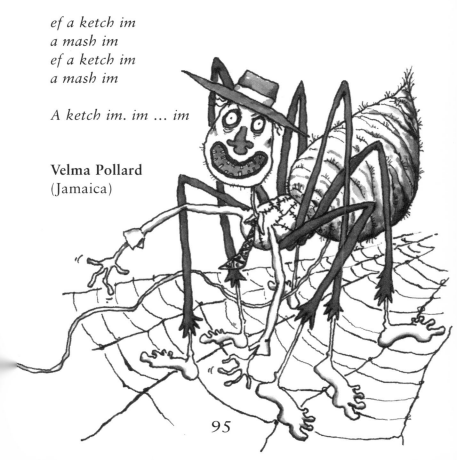

95

The Kangaroo

Old Jumpety-Bumpety-Hop-and-Go-One
Was lying asleep on his side in the sun.
This old kangaroo, he was whisking the flies
(With his long glossy tail) from his ears and his eyes.
Jumpety-Bumpety-Hop-and-Go-One
Was lying asleep on his side in the sun.
Jumpety-Bumpety-Hop!

Traditional
(Australia)

Kob Antelope

A creature to pet and spoil,
An animal with a smooth neck.
You live in the bush without getting lean.
You are plump like a newly wedded wife.
You have more brass rings round your neck
than any woman.

When you run you spread fine dust
like a butterfly shaking its wings.
You are beautiful like carved wood.
Your eyes are gentle like a dove's.
Your neck seems long, long
to the covetous eyes of the hunter.

Traditional Yoruba
(Nigeria)

The Elephant

The elephant
Is a variant
Of a colossus
That overpowers us
By its dignity
And its ability
To avoid smashing
Life. Never dashing
Through the dense
Forests – its senses
Alert to the smallest
Vibration, blest
With the patience
Of an ancient
Queen.

Bashabi Fraser
(India and UK)

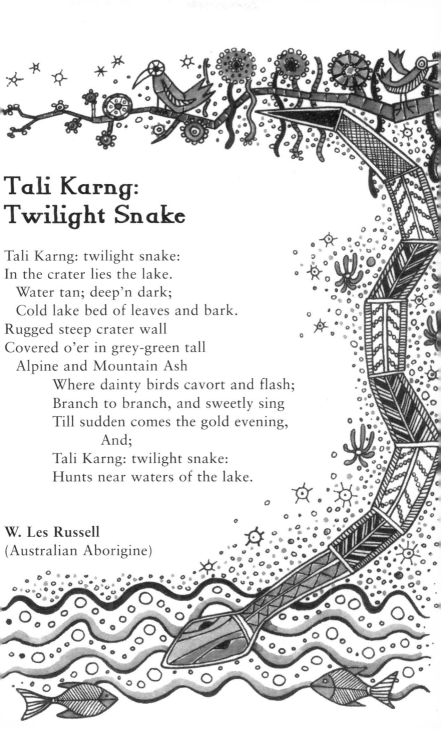

Tali Karng: Twilight Snake

Tali Karng: twilight snake:
In the crater lies the lake.
  Water tan; deep'n dark;
  Cold lake bed of leaves and bark.
Rugged steep crater wall
Covered o'er in grey-green tall
  Alpine and Mountain Ash
        Where dainty birds cavort and flash;
        Branch to branch, and sweetly sing
        Till sudden comes the gold evening,
              And;
        Tali Karng: twilight snake:
        Hunts near waters of the lake.

W. Les Russell
(Australian Aborigine)

The Monkey

Monkey, monkey, swinging high
In the treetops in the sky,
Are we brothers, are we one,
All together in the sun?

Who gave you that frame so frail?
Who made you that curling tail?
Why have you such puffy cheeks?
Why such scratches and such shrieks?

Do you wonder why the fuss?
Do you give a thought to us?
Funny, cute and somewhat queer,
Warm and furry, full of cheer.

When you leap from tree to tree
Are you glad that you are free?
You are nimble, you are quick,
You are up to every trick.

Human hands mark you our kin.
Monkey mischief makes us grin.
If I could I would erase
All the sadness from your gaze.

Monkey, monkey, swinging high
In the treetops in the sky,
We are brothers, everyone,
All together in the sun.

Debjani Chatterjee
(India and UK)

Note: This is a parody of William Blake's *The Tyger*.

EARTH CRIES

nature and environment

On the Road

Although they have tightly bound my arms and legs,
All over the mountains I hear the songs of birds,
And the forest is filled with the perfume of spring flowers.
Who can prevent me from freely enjoying these,
Which take from the long journey a little of its loneliness?

Ho Chi Minh
(Vietnam)
Translation

Autumn Song

The trees were on fire and the leaves rustled
a tune that only the listening mind can hear;
A song took wing and floated down on the arms
of the whistling wind:
I give you the gift of song, I give you the gift of fruit;
I give you the gift of healing, I give you the gift of dreams.
Only, take my gold, take my browns, take my mists,
take my winds and blend them into your autumn song ...

I rose as a phoenix amidst the clouds and
danced in joy with the laughing raindrops;
I shall take your gold, I shall take your browns,
I shall take your mists, I shall take your winds
and blend them into my autumn song ...

Then, your leaves shall heal, your gold shall soothe,
your fruits shall balm, your mists shall melt in dreams
and your winds shall whistle in hopes, when I sing
our autumn song ...

Usha Kishore
(India and UK)

Monsoon Moments
(a ghazal)

Once more the monsoon winds blow and I remember you;
Once more the leafy anklets chime and I remember you.

All day I was lost in the maze of worldly affairs;
Now when the sun climbs down the walls, I remember you.

Once more the crow calls in the empty courtyard at home,
Once more the drops of nectar fall – and I remember you.

Once more the herons cry in an ocean of green grass,
The season of yellow blooms has come – and I remember you.

At first I wept aloud, and then began to laugh.
Thunder rolls and lightning flashes – and I remember you.

Nasir Kazmi
(India and Pakistan)
Translated by Debjani Chatterjee

Note: A *ghazal* is a lyrical poem in couplets, originally in Arabic,
but popular in Urdu, Persian and other languages.

hurricane

first de earthquake come
shiver de house
like it wanna be dancing

nex day de wind roar
like dragons running

blow coconuts off tree
so dey bounce down street
like maracas start drumming

furniture lift up
high as quick run clouds

fix deyselves
in crook of cotton tree
an sit dere laughing

de ceiling of my house done fall
spoil de banana fudge
an downstairs fill like roaring river

we spend all night on de steeping stairs
play cards till i sleep
like letter N

on de morning after
de rickety houses
all flat so flat

look like de walls
done drop de trousers
run away

but roofs sit perfect
on de ground
still skirted for de dance

Caroline Carver
(Jamaica and UK)

How Do I Describe the Snow?

My cousins have asked me
To describe the snow
But I really don't know
How to tell them how
Softly it falls
How gently it fills
Our garden. How wet
It feels after it settles
On my shoulders
How freshly it crunches
Under my heels
How quickly it slides
Down a slippery bank
How thickly it lies
In the schoolyard
How easily it rolls
Into a ball
How swiftly it
Can shoot away
From my hand
And smash
Against my friend's back
To melt into powder
And be lost in the snow
On the playground!

Bashabi Fraser
(India and UK)

Sunset

The sun spun like
a tossed coin.
It whirled on the azure sky,
It clattered into the horizon,
It clicked in the slot,
And neon-lights popped
And blinked 'Time expired',
As on a parking meter.

Oswald Mbuyiseni Mtshali
(South Africa)

Prayer to the Moon

Take my face and give me yours!
Take my face, my unhappy face.
Give me your face,
with which you return
when you have died,
when you have vanished from sight.
You lie down and return –
Let me reassemble you, because you have joy,
you return evermore alive,
after you have vanished from sight.
Did you not promise us once
that we too should return
and be happy again after death?

Bushman
(Botswana)
Translation

earth cries

she doesn't cry for water
she runs rivers deep
she doesn't cry for food
she has suckled trees
she doesn't cry for clothing
she weaves all that she wears
she doesn't cry for shelter
she grows thatch everywhere
she doesn't cry for children
she's got more than she can bear
she doesn't cry for heaven
she knows it's always there
you don't know why she's crying
when she's got everything
how could you know she's crying
for just one humane being

Jean 'Binta' Breeze
(Jamaica and UK)

HOPSCOTCH

school and play

New Boy

Today
everyone is laughing
at your long name
and your skinny legs
which look like
two burnt out matches
but by next week
I bet
they'll be your friends.

Pauline Stewart
(Caribbean and UK)

Learning About Each Other

I am lucky to be in a school
with many different cultures.
I get on quite well with the
dark coloured girls in this
class. And some of the English
children are friendly and kind
to me and Hao. But some call
us names because we are
Chinese. But I don't care.
I am proud to be Chinese.
I am proud of my language.
Why don't we all learn about
each other and get on as
friends?

Hanh Tat
(Vietnam and UK)

Classes Under the Trees

My teacher, Mrs Zettie, says,
'Children, we can't breathe in here.
Come on! We're going
under the breadfruit tree!'

We leave the one room schoolhouse
these hot days in June
for the breeze outdoors
below blue skies.

Reciting our lessons
in singsong fashion,
we hear twittering birds
recite theirs, too.

Monica Gunning
(Jamaica and USA)

Me, the Whale and Gingernut

I walk to school alone. My uniform
is knitted and sewn
by Mum. If it rains
my skirt gets wet and smells
of old mushrooms
like the school.

Joan is my friend; they call her the whale
she helps me with my sums
I help her with art.
In the far corner of the playground
we tell each other stories.

Instinctively, kids are separated by rank, I'm
in the losers' group, with Joan. The brainy kids
sit on the wall below the Head's window and
wear badges so they can boss us about, while
the cool, hard kids keep everyone in their place.

I notice a new boy, targeted already.
Gingernut they're calling
because his hair is red.

Bright red, skin milk-white
long thin bones, pale blue eyes fringed
like sea anemones, brim with tears.
He passes me, moist-cheeked.

I reach out, warm him
with a smile; by next playtime
he is my friend.

A ruckus erupts in our corner, Joan
is pinned against the wall, a red slap
on her face. The girl I most fear
has her by the tie.

Her cardigan is in my hand
I am wrestling her
to the floor. We scratch, pull,
roll together. A steam train
in my head, then a scream; blood
on my hand.

All the kids have gathered round.
I see her groaning on the floor, clasping
her ear; in my hands a gold ring.
Gingernut is awestruck.

Kids talk to me differently now
or don't talk at all. Today
the hard girl decides
I can walk home with her, play
in the street. Joan hovers in the shade,
Gingernut tugs at my sleeve. A smile
starts in my head and freezes
on my lips. I'm going to be sick.

Gingernut is asking me to the cinema;
flouncing away I throw at him:

I don't go out with little boys!

Everyone laughs.
Gingernut's blue eyes become
glassy black. Starting at his throat
a tide of scarlet creeps toward his hair,
the lump in his throat
bobs up and down. Joan comes to him
with a gentle motion and they walk away.

I walk to school alone, I sit alone
while Gingernut sits with Joan.
The hard kids ignore me. Now everything
feels shabby; my home-made clothes,
the playground, the school, everything
is grey

like I am inside.

Contributors to *First Words*
(Various)

Note: *First Words* is a multilingual anthology produced by English-as-
a-second-language learners in Newcastle-upon-Tyne, UK.

Tables

Headmaster a come, Mek has'e! Sit down
– Amy! Min' yuh bruck Jane collar-bone,
Tom! Tek yuh foot off o' de desk,
Sandra Wallace, mi know yuh vex
But beg yuh get up off o' Joseph head.
Tek de lizard off o' Sue neck, Ted!
Sue, mi dear, don' bawl so loud;
Thomas, yuh can tell mi why yuh put de toad
Eena Elvira sandwich bag?
An Jim, whey yuh a do wid dat bull-frog?
Tek i' off mi table! Yuh mad?
Mi know yuh chair small, May, but it no dat bad
Dat yuh haffe siddung pon de floor!
Jim, don' squeeze de frog unda de door,
Put i' through de window – no, no, Les!
Mi know yuh hungry, but Mary yeas
Won' full yuh up, so spit it out.
Now go wash de blood outa yuh mout'.
Hortense, tek Mary to de nurse.
Nick, tek yuh han out o' Mary purse!
Ah wonda who tell all o' yuh
Sey dat dis classroom is a zoo?
Quick! Headmaster comin' through de door
'– *Two ones are two, two twos are four ...*'

Valerie Bloom
(Jamaica and UK)

Unlinked Arms

Splitting up with my best friend
was like shedding peas
from a pod
and popping them in
boiling water for a few minutes
It left me
with a soft wrinkled outer-coat
and hard inside.

Walking down
the broken hopscotch path
I reach the brook
where she had
mischievously thrown
the missing textbook
The delicious lie
we told the next day
mingles with the fogged
air of the past.

Splitting up with my best friend
I recall unshed tears
a Mona Lisa smile
and the brook
which carried my secrets
downstream
on rainy days.

What I remember most
are the unlinked arms
the unfollowed footsteps
And the solitary eating
of tuppenny liquorice.

Georgina Blake
(Caribbean and UK)

121

I Know the Answer

Sir – Sir
I've got my hand up Sir
I know the answer,
But once again the teacher
ignores my urgent plea,
That the answer to that question
Has got to be – minus three.

Sir I know the answer
His eyes glance above my head
Instead it's Tommy Tucker
who answers it instead.

Who was the first man on the moon?
Me Sir! Me Sir! I know! I know!
SIT QUIET BOY!
Stop jumping about ...
There is no need to shout
The question Mark, is not referred to you ...
Can you give me the answer Sue?
Clever girl – that is correct

NOW –
Who knows where the highest mountain in the world is?

Huh!
if he thinks I'm putting up my hand
he can get lost.
I won't give him the satisfaction of telling me to sit down –
OK Mark – what's the answer?
Mark! – wake up Mark!
In which country is the highest mountain?
Me Sir? Do you mean me Sir?
eh! eh!
I don't know Sir.

P. Omoboye
(UK)

Morning Break

Girls in white blouses, blue skirts,
boys in blue trousers, white shirts,
singing, swinging, screeching, reaching,
hooking wasps, riddle-saying,
ring-playing –
Bayhanna, bayhanna, bayhanna, bay –
If your teacher scolds you
listen to what you say
That's the way to bayhanna, bayhanna, bay.

Lamppost schoolmaster in grey jacket,
grey tale of wild Abaco hog and donkey;
mild worry, calm hurry,
stiff bones and cane;
ring-playing –
round the green apple tree
where the grass grows so sweet,
Miss Della Miss Della,
your true lover was here,
and he wrote you a letter
to turn 'round your head.

First bell, all frozen.
Second bell, instant motion,
Disappear.

Telcine Turner
(Bahamas)

I Wouldn't Go to Missie
(a clapping rhyme)

I wouldn't go to Missie
Any more, more, more
There's a big fat police
At the door, door, door

He will hold me by the collar
And make me pay a dollar
And a dollar is a dollar
So I wouldn't go to Missie
Any more, more, more

Traditional
(Caribbean)

Hopscotch

A hip hop hippity hop
yes it's time to play hopscotch
hip hop hippity hop
yes it's time to play hopscotch

a turn and a twist
we make a double fist
a jump and a spin
we go right in

a flop and a hop
I spin like a top
Jessie now stands upside down
her smile looks just like a frown

Hey!
a hip hop hippity hop
me and my friends play hopscotch
jumping
   laughing
      running
screaming
hip
   hop
      hippity
hop

we are all having fun
wanting to play till the day is done
until Gloria the big bully
comes and yells

BOYS DON'T PLAY HOPSCOTCH!!!

Afua Cooper
(Jamaica)

Eleven Years Old

I'm old enough
to work in the fields,
my grandmother says:
your limbs are young
and strong,
we need the extra hands
to tend the crop
and feed the goats
and till this ungrateful land.

Maybe
I'll go to school
when the crop is in,
when we take the few yams
from the soil,
then I'll wear a new dress,
and leave when it's early day
for it's only one mile to the school.

Dionne Brand
(Trinidad)

TREE IN THE HEART

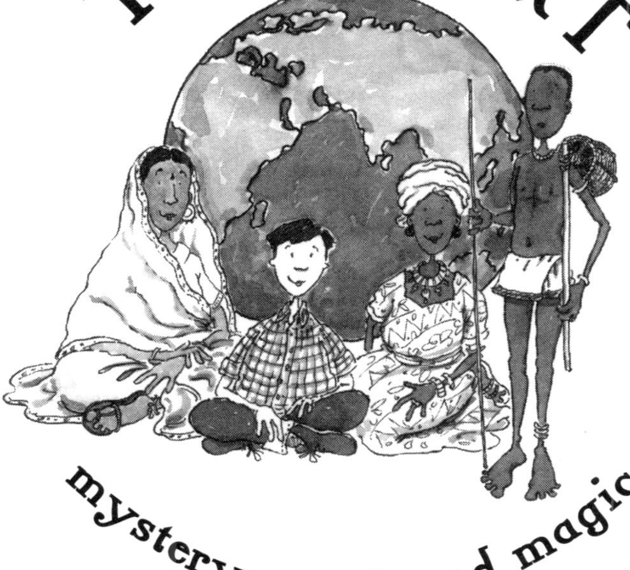

mystery, myth and magic

Mawu of the Waters

With mountains as my footstool
  and stars in my curls
I reach down to reap the waters with my fingers
and look! I cup lakes in my palms.
I fling oceans around me like a shawl
and am transformed
into a waterfall.
Springs flow through me
and spill rivers at my feet
as fresh streams surge to make seas.

Abena P. A. Busia
(Ghana)

Duppy Dance

You walk too-too late at night
duppies make your wrong road the right.
Around you, they rattle strings of bones.
And duppies dance. Duppies dance.

All along deep-deep dark road
duppies croak like one hidden mighty toad.
You hear scary bells toll.
And duppies dance. Duppies dance.

Duppies make horse-hooves clop-clop.
Make strange big birds flutter up.
Make you feel skin gone shrivelled.
And duppies dance. Duppies dance.

Roaring ten bulls like one bull
duppies rip off your clothes in one pull.
Skeletons prance around you.
And duppies dance. Duppies dance.

James Berry
(Jamaica and UK)

Note: *Duppy* is a Caribbean word
meaning 'a ghost'.

The Great Houdini
(a clerihew)

The Great Houdini,
like a mysterious genie,
vanished during his final act,
thus creating both legend and fact.

Debjani Chatterjee
(India and UK)

Note: A clerihew is a poem, in two rhyming couplets, about a famous person. The person's name is usually in the first line.

Superstition

I know
  That when a grumbling old woman
Is the first thing I meet in the morning
  I must rush back to bed
  And cover my head.
That wandering sheep on a sultry afternoon
Are really men come home from their dark graves
  To walk in light
  In mortal sight.
That when my left hand or eyelid twitches
Or when an owl hoots from a nearby tree
  I should need pluck,
  It means bad luck.
That drink spilled goes to ancestral spirits,
That witches dance in clumps of bananas;
That crumbs must be left in pots and plates
  Until the morn
  For babes unborn.
That it's wrong to stand in doorways at dusk
For the ghosts must pass – they have their right of way!
That when a hidden root trips me over
  Fault's not in my foot.
  It's an evil root.
That if I sleep with feet towards the door
  It'll not long be fit
  I know it – Yes I know it!

Minji Karibo
(Nigeria)

The Spider

I'm told that the spider
Has coiled inside her
Enough
Material
To spin an aerial
One-way track
To the moon and back;
Whilst I
Cannot even fly.

Frank Collymore
(Barbados)

The Star-Tribes

Look, among the boughs. Those stars are men.
There's Ngintu, with his dogs, who guards the skins
of Everlasting Water in the sky.
And there's the Crow-man, carrying on his back
the wounded Hawk-man. There's the Serpent, Thurroo,
glistening in the leaves. There's Kapeetah,
the Moon-man, sitting in his mia-mia.

And there's those Seven Sisters, travelling
across the sky. They make the real cold frost.
You hear them when you're camped out on the plains.
They look down from the sky and see your fire
and, 'Mai, mai, mai!' they sing out as they run
across the sky. And when you wake, you find
your swag, the camp, the plains all white with frost.

Related by Fred Biggs
(Australian Aborigine)

Corn and Potato

The corn and potato, peanut, strawberry:
Who gave them to us, can anyone tell me?
Canoes and snowshoes, hammocks for swinging:
Where did they come from in the beginning?

Was it Wonder Woman? No, No.
Six Million Dollar Man? No, No, No.
Was it Tom and Jerry? No, No.
Sylvester and Tweety? No, No, No.
Then was it Max B. Nimble? No, No.
Rocky and Bullwinkle? No, No, No.
Then was it Spiderman? No, No.
It must be Superman! No, No, No, No, No!

Next time you eat your strawberry jam
And peanuts, just ask your daddy this question,
Where did these come from: I'll give you one clue:
It wasn't Archie Bunker, that's all I can tell you.

Was it Paul Bunyon? No, No.
Was it Abraham Lincoln? No, No, No.
Francisco Pizarro? No, No.
Was it Robinson Crusoe? No, No, No.
Was it a Pilgrim Father? No, No.
Or an old fur trader? No, No, No.
Columbus or Champlain? No, No.
Tennille and the Captain? No, No, No.
I give up, won't you tell me? Yes, Yes, Yes, Yes, Yes!

If you can't guess then I'd better tell you.
Listen to me, I don't want to fool you.
Before Columbus, before the Pilgrims,
These things and more all came from the Indians.

The Mic-Mac, the Sarcee, Yes, Yes,
Ojibway and Plains Cree, Yes, Yes, Yes,
The Sioux and the Cheyenne, Yes, Yes,
Apache and Peigan, Yes, Yes, Yes,
The Arawak or Taino, Yes, Yes,
The Mapuche, the Saulteaux, Yes, Yes, Yes,
The Hopi, the Haida, Yes, Yes,
The Inca, the Maya, Yes, Yes, Yes, Yes, Yes!
(I said Yes! Yes! Yes!)

David Campbell
(Guyana)

Two Riddles

Green, green the plant;
Red, red my palm;
Gladdens my heart!

Stone among stones,
White and clear,
Made by heaven
And the Creator!

Traditional Arabic
(Yemen)
Translated by Debjani Chatterjee

Answers: henna, hailstones

Rain Magic

Gentle breeze is the father of rain,
Soft wind is the father of cloudburst.
Rain will not drench me today;
Rain will pack its belongings and go away.
  The antelope is humming,
  The buffalo is grumbling,
  The pig grunts in its belly.
Words have angered the red monkey,
But today he was given the right words
And his anger will disappear.

Traditional Yoruba
(Nigeria)
Translation

Untitled
(a haiku)

On the road through the clouds
Is there a short-cut
To the summer moon?

Den Sute-Jo
(Japan)
Translated by Kenneth Rexroth and Ikuko Atsumi

Tree in the Heart of the Void

The beginning was void. The first thing to be
formed in the heart of the void was a tree.
This first tree sprang out of a womb of energy,
and, emerging from its millions of buds, there
sprouted the whole of creation.

Traditional Maori
(creation myth from New Zealand)

THE LAST WORD

peace and harmony

I'd Like to Squeeze

I'd like to squeeze this round world
into a new shape

I'd like to squeeze this round world
like a tube of toothpaste

I'd like to squeeze this round world
fair and square

I'd like to squeeze this round world
till everybody had an equal share

John Agard
(Guyana and UK)

All I have

I never carried a rifle
On my shoulder
Or pilled a trigger.
All I have
Is a flute's melody
A brush to paint my dreams,
A bottle of ink.
All I have
Is unshakeable faith
And an infinite love
For my people in pain.

Tawfeeq Zayad
(Palestinian refugee)
Translation

An African Elegy

We are the miracles that God made
To taste the bitter fruit of Time.
We are precious
And one day our suffering
Will turn into the wonders of the earth.

There are things that burn me now
Which turn golden when I am happy.
Do you see the mystery of our pain?
That we bear poverty
And are able to sing and dream sweet things

And that we never curse the air when it is warm
Or the fruit when it tastes so good
Or the lights that bounce gently on the waters?
We bless things even in our pain.
We bless them in silence.

That is why our music is so sweet.
It makes the air remember.
There are secret miracles at work
That only Time will bring forth.
I too have heard the dead singing.

And they tell me that
This life is good
They tell me to live it gently
With fire, and always with hope.
There is wonder here

And there is surprise
In everything that moves unseen.
The ocean is full of songs.
The sky is not an enemy.
Destiny is our friend.

Ben Okri
(Nigeria and UK)

Note: An elegy is a poem or song of sorrow.

The Unknown You Have Made Known to Me

The unknown you have made known to me,
　In so many homes you gave me shelter.
You have brought the distant near, my friend,
　And made a brother of the stranger.

　　I fear to leave a place I know of old,
　　　Who knows what the future will unfold?
　　I forget the simple truth that within
　　　The new, you are the familiar.
　　You have brought the distant near, my friend,
　　　And made a brother of the stranger.

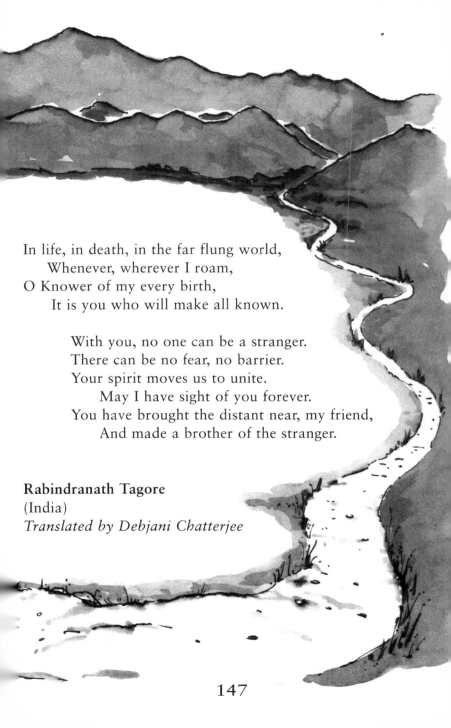

In life, in death, in the far flung world,
   Whenever, wherever I roam,
O Knower of my every birth,
   It is you who will make all known.

      With you, no one can be a stranger.
      There can be no fear, no barrier.
      Your spirit moves us to unite.
         May I have sight of you forever.
      You have brought the distant near, my friend,
         And made a brother of the stranger.

Rabindranath Tagore
(India)
Translated by Debjani Chatterjee

Red

Red is the colour
of my Blood;
of the earth,
of which I am a part;
of the sun as it rises, or sets,
of which I am a part;
of the blood
of the animals,
of which I am a part;
of the flowers, like the waratah,
of the twining pea,
of which I am a part;
of the blood of the tree
of which I am a part.
For all things are a part of me,
and I am a part of them.

W. Les Russell
(Australian Aborigine)

Note: A waratah is a red flower. It is the emblem of
New South Wales in Australia.

The Wheel Around the World

If all the world's children
wanted to play holding hands
they could happily make
a wheel around the seas.

If all the world's children
wanted to play holding hands
they could be sailors
and build a bridge across the seas.

What a beautiful chorus we would make
singing around the earth
if all the humans in the world
wanted to dance holding hands!

Traditional
(Mozambique)

INDEX OF FIRST LINES

INDEX OF AUTHORS

Acknowledgements

The editors and the Publisher would like to thank the following for permission to include the following poems in this collection:

John Agard for 'I'd Like to Squeeze', published in *Get Back, Pimple!* by Viking Kestrel; 'Hippo Writes a Love Poem to his Wife' published in *We Animals Would Like a Word With You* by Random House Children's Books; and 'Windrush Welcome' at www.bbc.co.uk/education/windrush/

Shafi Ahmed for 'Bulu's Freedom', published in *The Redbeck Anthology of British South Asian Poetry* by Redbeck Press.

Ama Ata Aidoo for 'The Birthday Gift', published in *An Angry Letter in January* by Dangaroo Press.

Moniza Alvi for 'Arrival 1946', published in *Carrying my Wife* by Bloodaxe.

Su Andi for 'Truth', published in *Nearly Forty* by Spike Books.

James Berry for 'Postcard Poem: Solo', published in *The Word Party* by Macmillan Children's Books; and 'Duppy Dance', published in *Unzip Your Lips* by Macmillan Children's Books.

Fred Biggs for 'The Star-Tribes', published in *New Oxford Book of Australian Verse* by OUP Melbourne.

Georgina Blake for 'Who Sings for Fathers?' and 'Unlinked Arms', both published in *The Delicious Lie* by Crocus Books.

Valerie Bloom for 'Water Everywhere', published in *Can I Buy a Slice of Sky?: Poems from Black, Asian and American Indian Cultures* by Blackie and Sons; and 'Tables', published in *Duppy Jamboree* by Cambridge University Press.

Dionne Brand for 'Eleven Years Old', published in *Can I Buy a Slice of Sky?: Poems from Black, Asian and American Indian Cultures* by Blackie and Sons.

Jean 'Binta' Breeze for 'earth cries' published in *The Arrival of Brighteye* by Bloodaxe and 'For The Mother', from *Everybody's Mother* edited by Linda Coggin and Clare Marlow, published by Peterloo Poets.

Jean Buffong for 'Dance', published in *Hearsay: Performance Poems Plus* by The Bodley Head.

Bushman (Botswana) for 'Prayer to the Moon', published in *Growing up with Poetry: An Anthology for Secondary Schools* by Heinemann International.

Abena P. A. Busia for 'Mawu of the Waters', published in *Around the World in Eighty Days* by Macmillan Children's Books.

David Campbell for 'Corn and Potato', published in *Can I Buy a Slice of Sky?: Poems from Black, Asian and American Indian Cultures* by Blackie and Sons.

Caroline Carver for 'uncle boatman' and 'Hurricane', both published in *Jingharzi an' me* by Semicolon.

J. H. Chaplin for 'Town and Village', published in *A Child's Book of African Poetry: An Anthology for Upper Primary Schools* by Macmillan.

Debjani Chatterjee for 'All in the Name', published in *I'm in a Mood Today* by Oxford University Press; 'The Great Houdini'; 'The Monkey', published in *Animal Antics* by Pennine Pens; 'Treat of a Sweet', published in *The Great Escape* by Macmillan Children's Books; her translation of 'The Savan Festival'; her translation of Nasir Kazmi's 'Monsoon Moments' (a ghazal), published in *The Unidentified Frying Omelette* by Hodder Wayland; her translation of Rabindranath Tagore's 'The Unknown You have Made Known to Me', published in *Lodestones* by The Border Poets; and her translation of 'Two Riddles', published in *Who Cares? Reminiscences of Yemeni Carers in Sheffield* by Sheffield Carers Centre.

Merle Collins for 'Same but different', published in *Watchers & Seekers* by The Women's Press.

Frank Collymore for 'The Spider' and 'Phiniphin', both published in *A Caribbean Dozen: Poems from Caribbean Poets* by Walker Books.

Afua Cooper for 'Hopscotch', published in *Poems About School* by Hodder Wayland Publishers.

Fred D'Aguiar for 'Airy Hall Iconography', published in *Big World, Little World* by Nelson.

David Diop for 'Africa', published in *Growing up with Poetry: An Anthology for Secondary Schools* by Heinemann International.

Jeanne Ellin for 'Grandmother', published in *The Redbeck Anthology of British South Asian Poetry* by Redbeck Press.

Knolly La Fortune for 'Carnival Rhapsody', published in *Voice Print: An Anthology of Oral and Related Poetry* from the Caribbean by Longman.

Bashabi Fraser for 'Between my two Worlds', published in *Wish I Was Here* by Pocketbooks; 'The Elephant'; 'Curry Call'; 'How do I describe the snow?'; and 'A Card for Me Mom'.

Martin Glynn for 'Genius', published in *Unzip Your Lips Again* by Macmillan Children's Books.

Lorna Goodison for 'Some of my Worst Wounds', published in *Heartsease* by New Beacon Books.

Nirmalendu Goon for 'February', published in *From Briarwood to Barishal to Bricklane.*

Monica Gunning for 'Classes Under the Trees', published in *Poems About School* by Hodder Wayland.

A. L. Hendriks for 'What Colour is a Kiss?' published in *To Speak Simply* by Hippopotamus Press.

Mahmood Jamal for 'Migrants', published in *The Redbeck Anthology of British South Asian Poetry* by Redbeck Press.

Meiling Jin for 'World Geography and the Rainbow Alliance', published in *Black Women Talk Poetry* by Blackwoman Talk.

Amryl Johnson for 'Traveller's Prayer', published in *Gorgons* by Cofa Press.

Sajed Kamal for his translation of Begum Sufia Kamal's 'There's This Goat', published in *Mother of Pearls and other Poems* by Bangla Academy.

Minji Karibo for 'Superstition', published in *Someone is Flying Balloons: Australian Poems for Children* by Omnibus Books.

Amin Kassam for 'Trapped in a puddle', published in *Someone is Flying Balloons: Australian Poems for Children*, Omnibus Books.

Jackie Kay for 'Brendon Gallacher', published in *Two's Company* by Blackie Books.

Usha Kishore for 'Autumn Song', published in *Countryside Tales – Autumn* 2000.

Robert Lee for 'Mango', published in *Around the World in Eighty Days* by Macmillan Children's Books.

Bekleen Leong for 'The Perfectly Baked Cakes', published in *Black Women Talk Poetry* by Blackwoman Talk.

John Lyons for 'Bobolee', published in *The Sun Rises in the North* by Smith Doorstop Books; 'Adventurer', published in *On a Camel to the Moon* by Belitha Press.

Irfan Merchant for 'Tableau', published in *The Redbeck Anthology of British South Asian Poetry* by Redbeck Press.

Thomas Merton for his translation of Chuang Tzu's 'The Joy of Fishes', published in *The Way of Chuang Tzu* by New Directions Publishing Corporation.

Ho Chi Minh for 'On the Road', published in *One for Blair* by Young World Books.

Moritake for 'Untitled' (a haiku), published in *The Unidentified Frying Omelette* by Hodder Wayland.

Oswald Mbuyiseni Mtshali for 'Sunset', published in *Poems of Black Africa* by Secker and Warburg.

Grace Nichols for 'Skanking Englishman between Trains', published in *The Fat Black Woman's Poems* by Virago; and 'Tapestry', published in *Lazy Thoughts of a Lazy Woman* by Virago.

Oodgeroo Noonuccal (Kath Walker) for 'Corroboree', published in *Someone is Flying Balloons: Australian Poems for Children* by Omnibus Books.

A. K. Nyabongo for 'Mother Parrot's Advice to her Children', published in *Big World, Little World* by Nelson.

Odia Ofeimun for 'Landing on the Moon', published in *Poems of Black Africa* by Secker & Warburg.

Gabriel Okara for 'Once Upon a Time', published in *Growing up with Poetry: An Anthology for Secondary Schools* by Heinemann International.

Ben Okri for 'African Elegy', published in *An African Elegy* by Jonathon Cape.

P. Omoboye for 'I Know the Answer', published in *Can I Buy a Slice of Sky?: Poems from Black, Asian and American Indian Cultures* by Blackie and Sons.

Tao Lang Pee for 'Sampan', published in *Can I Buy a Slice of Sky?: Poems from Black, Asian and American Indian Cultures* by Blackie.

Velma Pollard for 'The Fly', published in *Voice Print: An Anthology of Oral and Related Poetry from the Caribbean* by Longman.

William Radice for his translation of Rabindranath Tagore's 'Too long I've wandered', published in *Rabindranath Tagore: Particles, Jottings, Sparks – The Collected Brief Poems* by Angel Books.

Kuini Mohehau Reedy for 'My Loved One', published in *Penguin Book of Contemporary New Zealand Poetry: Nga Kupu Titohu o Aotearoa* by Penguin Auckland.

Kenneth Rexroth & Ikuko Atsumi for their translations of Den Sute-Jo's 'Untitled' (a haiku), and Okamoto Kanoko's 'All day long ...' (a tanka), both published in *Women Poets of Japan* by New Directions Book, New York, and Penguin Books Canada.

Sista Roots for 'Their Plan', published in *Watchers & Seekers* by The Women's Press.

Lucinda Roy for 'a 'coloured' girl, I sleep with rainbows', published in *Wailing the Dead to Sleep*.

158

W. Les Russell for 'Red' and 'Tali Karng: Twilight Snake', published in *Inside Black Australia: An Anthology of Aboriginal Poetry* by Penguin Books Australia.

Lemn Sissay for 'Airmail to a Dictionary', published in *Unzip Your Lips* by Macmillan Children's Books.

Hamid Shami for 'Mother Tongue', published in *Wish I Was Here* by Pocketbooks.

Pauline Stewart for 'New Boy', published in *Poems About School* by Hodder Wayland.

Hanh Tat for 'Learning About Each Other', published in *Peaces: Poems for Peace by Sheffield Schoolchildren* by Sheffield Racial Equality Council & Sheffield Education Department.

Traditional Australian for 'The Kangaroo', published in *Come to the Carnival: Festival Poems* by Oxford University Press.

Traditional Caribbean for 'I wouldn't go to Missie', published in *No Hickory, No Dickory, No Dock: A Collection of Caribbean Nursery Rhymes* by Viking Penguin.

Traditional Dinka for 'The Magnificent Bull', published in *Trade Winds* by Longman.

Traditional Maori for 'Tree in the Heart of the Void', published in *Big World, Little World* by Nelson.

Traditional Mozambique for 'The Wheel Around the World', published in *Around the World in Eighty Days* by Macmillan Children's Books.

Traditional Yoruba for 'Rain Magic', published in Big World, Little World by Nelson; and 'Kob Antelope' published in *A Child's Book of African Poetry: An Anthology for Upper Primary Schools* by Macmillan.

Telcine Turner for 'Morning Break', published in *Can I Buy a Slice of Sky?: Poems from Black, Asian and American Indian Cultures* by Blackie and Sons.

Chuang Tzu for 'The Joy of Fishes', published in *Can I Buy a Slice of Sky?: Poems from Black, Asian and American Indian Cultures* by Blackie and Sons.

Derek Walcott for 'Midsummer, Tobago', published in *Sea Grapes* by Jonathan Cape.

Contributors to *First Words* for 'Me, the Whale and Gingernut', published in *First Words* by First Step.

Ke Yan for 'Isn't It ...', published in *Around the World in Eighty Days* by Macmillan Children's Books.

Tawfeeq Zayad for 'All I Have', published in *Poets for Peace* by Edinburgh Stop the War Coalition.

Benjamin Zephaniah for 'Who's Who', published in *Shorts* by Macmillan Children's Books; and 'Body Talk', published in *Unzip Your Lips* by Macmillan Children's Books.

All possible care has been taken to trace the ownership of each poem in this selection and to obtain copyright permission for its use. If there are any omissions or if any errors have occurred, they will be corrected in subsequent editions, on notification to the Publishers.

159

About the Editors

Debjani Chatterjee and Bashabi Fraser are Indian-born writers who live in Sheffield and Edinburgh. They have exotic husbands (Debjani's is Brian and Bashabi's is Neil) and share a passion for poetry, cats and marmalade. Some people think they are twins.

Debjani went to school and university in India, Japan, Bangladesh, Hong Kong, Egypt and England. She has worked in the steel industry and in community relations, and been a teacher and lecturer. Debjani is now a full-time writer/storyteller who enjoys working with children. She has written, edited and translated over 30 books.

Bashabi moved between India and Britain for her school and university education. She teaches English Literature in two British universities. Bashabi has written, translated and edited poems, stories and articles for several books. She loves doing poetry and dance workshops and storytelling sessions with children and her daughter Rupsha shares Bashabi's love of performing Indian classical dance.